OREGON

A Turner Educational Services, Inc. book. Based on the Portrait
of America television series created by R.E. (Ted) Turner.

Library of Congress Number: 85-9973

34567890   908988

Library of Congress Cataloging in Publication Data

Thompson, Kathleen.
  Oregon.

  (Portrait of America)
  "A Turner book."
  Summary: Discusses the history, economy, culture,
and future of Oregon. Also includes a state
chronology, pertinent statistics, and maps.
  1. Oregon—Juvenile literature. [1. Oregon]
I. Title. II. Series: Thompson, Kathleen. Portrait of
America.
F876.3.T46   1985   979.5   85-9973
ISBN 0-86514-441-9 (lib. bdg.)
ISBN 0-86514-516-4 (softcover)

Cover Photo: USDA Forest Service, Photo by Jim Hughes

★ ★ ★ ★ ★
Portrait of AMERICA

OREGON

Kathleen Thompson

A TURNER BOOK
RAINTREE PUBLISHERS

CONTENTS

Introduction

Oregon, wilderness paradise.

"From what I've seen of the rest of the United States and Mexico, I think that it's really hard to find a state that has the amount of majesty that this place does, and is still so livable."

Oregon: forests, mountains, dams, shopping, and Shakespeare.

"When I met my husband, we drove cross-country. And of all the states that we've ever been in, this is where I chose to live. And I wouldn't move out of this state for anything. I love it up here."

Oregon is considered one of the most livable states in the country. It has more than its share of natural beauty and natural resources. The people of Oregon have worked to preserve their clean air and clean water. At the same time, there is industry in Oregon, and growth.

Oregon is a state where it's still possible to dream of a perfect place for people to live. But Oregon could change quickly if care is not taken. How the people of this so nearly perfect state meet that challenge is the story of Oregon.

The Haceta Head lighthouse in Florence.

Behind the Columbia Bar

Columbus discovered America in 1492. Spanish explorers traveled up into Texas and New Mexico in the early 1500s. But no European set foot on the land of Oregon until almost three hundred years later.

Chinook Indians were still fishing for salmon in the lower Columbia River when colonists in Boston were throwing tea into the bay. The Bannock, Cayuse, Paiute, Umatilla, and Nez Percé still lived peacefully on the desert east of the Cascade Mountains when the Declaration of Independence was being signed. The Klamath and Modoc Indians, and the Clackama, Multnomah, and Tillamook tribes were all hunting in the forests of Oregon when thirteen small colonies on the east coast became the United States of America.

The Snake River in Hells Canyon.

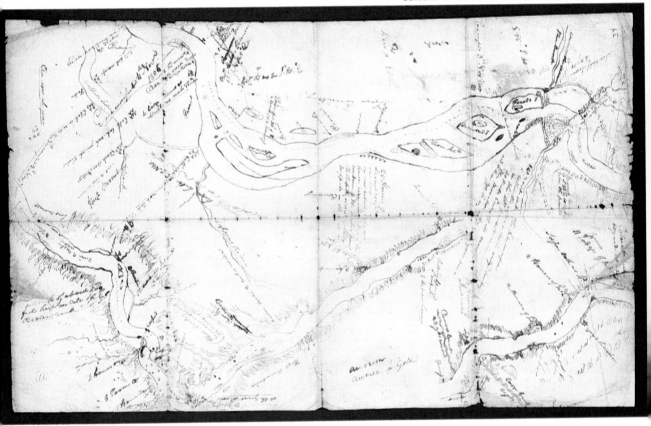

Above is a photograph of the actual map used by Lewis and Clark when they explored Oregon. During the winter, they stayed at Fort Clatsop (left).

Oregon was well-protected from traders, trappers, and explorers. Between this wild land and the first American settlers were high, icy mountains, wide prairies, raging rivers. Approaching by sea was no easier. The shores were dangerous, lined with shifting sands. The waters were churned by high winds.

Spanish sailors saw the Oregon coast on their way from Mexico to the Philippines in the 1500s and 1600s. Sir Francis Drake, the famous English explorer, may have touched the coast in 1579. Like many others, he was searching for a way from the northern Pacific Ocean to the Atlantic. But it wasn't until 1778 that James Cook reached Cape Foulweather near Yaquina Bay. The name he gave the cape tells us what he thought of it.

In 1788, the first American reached the Oregon shore. His name was Robert Gray. Four years later, he sailed up the Columbia River, naming it for his ship. The same year, 1792, George Vancouver, an English sailor, explored the coast and made maps.

Oregon wasn't reached by land until 1805. In that year, Meriwether Lewis and William Clark went as far as the mouth of the Columbia River.

In the early 1800s, the area that was called the Oregon region stretched from Alaska to California and from the Pacific Ocean to the Rocky Mountains. Four countries claimed parts of the region.

Russia said that it should have the land because of Russian explorations along the northern coast of the Pacific. But then, in 1824 and 1825, Russia signed treaties with the United States and Great Britain giving up all its claims to land south of latitude 54° 40'. Later, that latitude would become very famous.

In 1819, Spain gave up its claim to any land north of latitude 42°. That is now the border between Oregon and California.

That took care of two of the countries. But the United States and Great Britain couldn't agree on a way to split the land between them. So they signed a treaty that said that citizens of both countries could settle in the region. That put off for a while the day when an agreement would have to be reached.

White settlement of Oregon began with John Jacob Astor, an American fur trader. In 1811, he opened a fur-trading post. In 1825, the Hudson's Bay Company set up Fort Vancouver near the Columbia River. The Hudson's Bay was a large and very powerful British trading company. John McLoughlin was put in charge. He governed the region for about twenty years. He was British, but he later became a U.S. citizen. He is sometimes called the Father of Oregon.

When American settlers came to Oregon, they headed straight for the Willamette Valley. A lot of Oregon is covered with majestic mountains and dramatic deserts. But this narrow strip of land just west of the Cascade Mountains is a fertile valley, perfect for farming. Methodist missionaries were the first to start a permanent settlement in the valley, in 1834.

Then, in 1843, about a thousand settlers traveled the Oregon Trail to the Willamette Valley. From that time on, hundreds of settlers came every year.

Pretty soon, it became clear that Great Britain and the United States had to decide who was going to govern the region. There were just too many people building homes and farms. And, the American settlers wanted to be sure they were going to

be living on American soil.

In 1844, James K. Polk ran for president. In his campaign, he promised to get the land south of latitude 54° 40' for the United States. His slogan was "Fifty-four Forty or Fight."

Polk was elected president, and in 1846 he signed a treaty with Great Britain. It was a compromise. The United States would have the land south of 49° latitude. Great Britain would have the land above it.

Below is one of the kinds of Oregon terrain settlers crossed on their way west. John McLoughlin (right) helped people settle in the Willamette Valley area. His home (above, right) is now a historic site.

USDA Forest Service, Photo by Jim Hughes

These two nineteenth-century photographs show Chief Joseph (left) and an Indian using a spear to fish for salmon.

All the time that the United States and the European countries were arguing about who owned the Oregon region, the original owners were still there. In 1847, fighting between the Indians and white settlers became fierce. That year, Indians killed fourteen people near Walla Walla, Washington. The settlers fought back and the Cayuse War began. Many Indian villages were destroyed.

In the 1850s, the Indians again became angry at being driven from their lands. The Rogue River Wars began. In 1856, their leader, Chief John, surrendered and was put in prison.

In 1872, white settlers tried to force the Modoc Indians onto the Klamath Indian reservation. But the Indians hid out in lava beds. The land protected them, making a natural defense against attackers. One thousand U.S. soldiers were sent to force the Indians out. And a small band of Indian warriors kept them at bay from November 1872 until June 1873. In the end, the Indians surrendered.

The Nez Percé Indians lived in the beautiful Wallowa Valley. In 1877, the U.S. government tried to move them to a reservation in Idaho. But the Nez Percé refused to leave their home. Again, the army was sent in. Chief Joseph fought a gallant war, but he, too, was defeated. He was captured near the Canadian border and surrendered.

The Paiute and Bannock Indians tried to fight American settlers in 1878. They were defeated.

In the meantime, the settlers were beginning to set up a government. They met in 1843 and adopted a set of laws based on the laws of Iowa. Oregon became a territory in 1848. Oregon City was the capital. In 1859, the capital was moved to Salem.

The present boundaries of the state of Oregon were established in 1853.

There was one law that was very important in the growth of Oregon. It was called the Donation Land Law. This law said that any male American citizen who settled in Oregon before December 1850 could receive 320 acres of land. His wife could receive the same. Then he had to work his land for four years before he owned it. After December 1850 and before 1855, a settler had to be twenty-one years old, not eighteen, to get the land and he got only 160 acres. This law brought hundreds of settlers into the area.

And it soon was a state. Oregon became the thirty-third state in 1859. Salem was the state capital and John Whiteaker was the first governor.

During the Civil War, U.S. soldiers were not available to protect the settlers, so state

volunteers had to do the job. After the war ended, men who had fought on both sides came to Oregon looking for new opportunities. Between 1860 and 1890, the population of Oregon climbed from 52,000 to 300,000.

In the early part of the twentieth century, two very important things happened in Oregon politics. In 1902, Oregon adopted procedures that let the voters participate directly in making laws for their state. Then, in 1908, as part of the same reform movement, the state adopted *recall*—a way to remove people from public office if they were considered undesirable.

The other important political movement at this time was women's rights. Perhaps because the frontier woman was so much a part of the struggle to settle the West, several of the western states were ahead of the eastern states in recognizing the rights of women. In Oregon, the movement was led by Abigail Jane Scott Duniway. It was a long and difficult fight. But, in 1912, Oregon gave women the right to vote.

In the 1930s the Great Depression hit the country. One of the ways the federal government fought the depression was to provide money for public works. In Oregon, the government paid for the construction of the Bonneville Dam on the Columbia River. This dam provided electricity for industry. The Owyhee Dam, which was finished in 1932, helped irrigate large areas of farmland in the Owyhee and Snake river valleys.

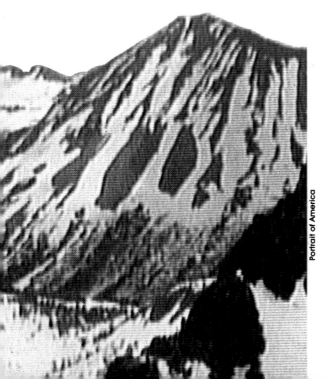

Portrait of America

Abigail Jane Scott Duniway (far left) and a view of the Cascade Mountains.

The Second World War brought another wave of people into Oregon. People who came to Oregon to work in the state's many defense plants liked what they saw and stayed. Besides these factories that produced military equipment, Oregon had other things to offer the war effort. Portland became an important port city. Supplies were shipped from there to soldiers in the Pacific and to our ally, Russia.

During the 1950s, two more big dams were built in Oregon— the McNary and the Dalles. They provided more clean, low-cost electric power for the state. Then, pipelines brought natural gas into Oregon for the first time. Industry grew. People began to move from the country to the city to work in factories.

Logging had always been a major industry in Oregon. In the 1960s, there were a lot of changes in logging. People became more aware of how valuable the trees were. And they began to realize that the forests would not last forever. So the logging industry started planting more trees to replace the ones that were cut

down. And the industry started using every bit of the tree. Before, bark and sawdust and wood chips had been thrown away. Now, nothing was wasted.

As industry grew, the people of Oregon began to be concerned that their beautiful state would be ruined by progress. Tom McCall, governor of the state from 1967 to 1975, led a movement to preserve the natural wonders of Oregon. Some of

The McNary Dam, on the Columbia River at Umatilla.

the country's best conservation laws were passed in Oregon in the 1960s and 1970s.

In 1964, terrible floods hit the state. They caused millions of dollars of damage. Some people were killed. Thousands were forced from their homes.

In the 1970s, Oregon built two more dams on its mighty rivers. The rivers are one of the reasons that Oregon can continue to provide energy for its people without the air pollution problems that are caused by coal and oil. But the demand for energy has grown to the point that some power plants now run on coal. Also, nuclear energy plants have recently been built.

Once Oregon's beauty was protected by its dangerous coastline and its rugged mountains. Today its only protection is the people who live in Oregon and love it.

One Man's Fight

"I simply say that Oregon is demure and lovely, that it ought to play a little hard to get. And I think you'll be just as sick as I am if we find it's nothing but a hungry hussy, throwing herself at every stinking smokestack that's offered."

Oregon is a beautiful place, a land of wilderness long after most of this country has been tamed by roads and railways. But can you stand in the way of progress? One man in Oregon thought so. His name was Tom McCall.

Tom McCall was a journalist. He was also once governor of Oregon. And he wanted Oregon to remain beautiful. He didn't want to see its natural wonders destroyed by dirty air, dirty water, and ruined land. So he fought for laws that would protect the land. He told people to come to Oregon to visit . . . but not to stay.

" . . . It was conflicting with the image of hospitality a governor's supposed to have. And western hospitality is equated with God and motherhood. But it started a lot of people thinking about growth."

National Park Services

In part because of Tom McCall, Oregon has passed the best laws designed to protect the environment of any state in the country. Three hundred and fifty miles of coastline have been protected by law. You can't sell no-deposit soft-drink bottles and cans in Oregon. There's a commission to see that there will always be farmland and wilderness even while land is being used for factories and the lumber industry.

But the fight—Tom McCall's fight—is not over. Progress means more jobs and more money. And the people of Oregon—like people everywhere—want those things. Protecting the land and air and water is something that has to go on day by day.

Before he died of cancer, Tom McCall spoke up one more time.

"I just feel that I don't have the time to stick around and give everybody hell for doing the wrong things. I've got to do all I can right now. This may sound corny, but this activist loves Oregon more than life.

"But if the legacy we have helped give Oregon, and which made it twinkle afar—what if it goes? I guess I wouldn't want to live in Oregon anyhow."

It's not a simple question. There has to be a balance between protecting nature and serving the people who live in the state. So far, Oregon has been doing a good job of finding its balance. For the sake of the whole country, let's hope it can continue.

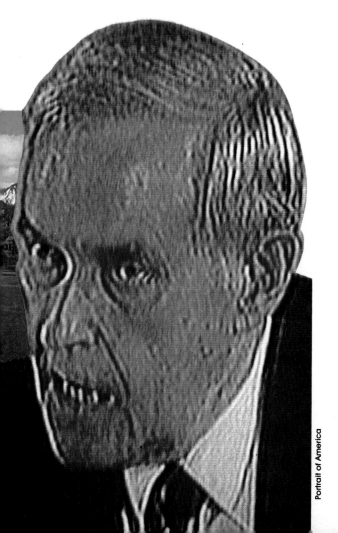

Portrait of America

Former governor Tom McCall is shown against a background of some of the beautiful Oregon land he fought to protect.

The Giving Land

In Oregon, the land is generous. It gives the people the great forests of the Cascade Mountains. It offers the fertile farmland of the Willamette Valley. West of the Cascades, there is more water than the farmers of the dry southwestern states could even dream about. East of the mighty mountains, there are vast ranges where cattle can graze.

Almost 80 percent of the goods produced in Oregon are manufactured products. But the manufacturing is based on raw materials from the land.

The most important industry in Oregon is wood processing. Oregon is the leading lumber producer in the entire country. It provides about one-fourth of the country's supply of lumber every year—7.5 billion board feet. It also

The Wallowa Mountains.

produces 40 percent of the nation's supply of plywood. Almost every city in Oregon has sawmills or plants that make products from wood.

All of these wood products come from the forests of Oregon. There are 30 million acres of forest in the state. Most of that is commercial forestland. Most of the trees are either Douglas fir or ponderosa pine.

The second largest industry in

Oregon is food processing. Again, the raw materials come from the state itself. Factories in the state process more than forty Oregon crops. In the Willamette Valley, there are canneries and freezing plants that pack fruit and vegetables from the area. There are also meat-processing plants in this region. In Astoria, plants pack fish and shellfish. Cities on the coast and along the Columbia River process seafood.

The third-ranking industry takes us back to the forests. It is paper products. Paper mills in Oregon produce more than three million tons of paper every year. In addition, they produce almost the same amount of paper pulp.

After manufacturing comes agriculture. The state of Oregon has over 30,000 farms. They are not large, averaging about 600 acres.

The most valuable crop is wheat, grown east of the Cascade Mountains. Hay is grown to feed livestock. Other grain crops are barley and oats.

Oregon grows some interesting and unusual crops. And some beautiful ones. For example, Oregon grows bulbs, the kind you plant.

In parts of western Oregon, you'll see fields of daffodils, gladioli, irises, lilies, and tulips. Farmers harvest the bulbs from these fields and ship them around the country to be planted in backyard gardens.

Oregon Economic Development Department

The photographs show three of Oregon's major industries: a paper mill (above, left), a food processing plant (far left), and a farm that grows wheat (near left).

25

A pole-bean farm in the Willamette Valley.

Oregon farmers also produce grass seed. They provide most of the country's supply of seed for such unusual plants as bent, fescue, ryegrass, common vetch, crimson clover, and merion bluegrass.

Oregon is one of the leading producers of peppermint.

The Willamette Valley is a vegetable garden. The fields are full of snap beans, green peas, onions, and sweet corn. Irrigated lands to the east are used for potatoes and sugar beets.

And then there is fruit. Oregon pears are famous. The Hood River Valley is a center for apples. The western and northern counties give us peaches, plums, prunes, and sweet cherries. Oregon is a leading strawberry-producing state. Other berries that are grown in Oregon

The trees on this nut farm are being sprayed with a pesticide.

include cranberries, blackberries, blueberries, boysenberries, gooseberries, loganberries, and raspberries.

Oregon also produces one of the country's biggest nut crops.

On the less fertile land east of the Cascade Mountains, beef cattle are raised. They are Oregon's most important livestock.

Finally, Oregon has small but important mineral and fishing industries.

All in all, Oregon is a state of rich variety. In other places, people have to coax and pamper the land. Here, although the farmers and loggers and other laborers work hard, the land itself is generous. And the biggest job of the people of Oregon is to respect, not abuse, its generosity.

Tree Cutters and Tree Planters

"You're out there in the elements and some days the sun shines and sometimes it's raining, and then it's snowin' and blowin' and next day it's hotter than . . . really hot. So, you just gotta love the outdoors or you don't want to be a logger . . . ."

A lot of Oregon is covered with trees. Forty percent of the state is commercial forest. Or, to look at it another way, one out of five commercial trees in the country grows in this state. And lumber is very important to the economy of Oregon.

So the trees are cut. And the loggers are there to cut them. They work hard days, and dangerous ones, in the out-of-doors, in the forests that they love—and cut down.

"I'd kind of like to use that as a comparison with what we're doing here to what each of us do at home in our garden, you know. We till the soil, we work it up. We plant our garden in the spring and it comes up and it gets green and it matures. And so when it matures, we don't just look at it and admire it. We go out and pick the tomatoes, we use it. Just like a garden. It just takes a little longer."

Actually, it takes a lot longer. A tree that has gone to make two-by-fours, books, and pencils may have been growing in the forest for a century or two. And it will take that long for another tree to grow and replace it.

At the far left is one of Oregon's loggers. Two loggers (above, left) are beginning to cut down a huge tree. At the left, logs are being prepared to be taken to a mill.

In Oregon, fortunately for the future, there will *be* trees to walk under, gaze at, and cut down a century from now. The loggers are not the only workers in the forest. There are the hoedads, too.

"You know, you plant a tree by every stump, so you do feel like you're putting the woods back. And when you go back to a stand where you planted two or three years, four or five years ago, then you feel like, yeah, it's coming back."

The hoedads are the country's largest tree-planting cooperative. Men, women, and children— they live most of the year in the

Ed Farren

forest. It's not an easy life, and planting hundreds of thousands of trees every year is not an easy job.

"You have to have good adrenal glands to get it pumpin'. You have to have endurance. It gets hot out here, it's dusty, or it's real rainy and miserable, so there's a certain perseverance, a certain roughness."

The first tree-planters were drifters. They worked too hard for too little money. But now, the workers have organized into cooperatives. They work together to make their jobs and their lives better.

The tree cutters and the tree planters, both important parts of Oregon today.

"It's not like, you know, 'the loggers are the bad guys and the tree planters are the good guys' kind of thing. It's just what we do for a living."

Paul Bunyan is alive and well and living in Oregon. And so is Johnny Appleseed.

These three photographs show hoedads. Each year the hoedads plant hundreds of thousands of trees to replace those that are cut down for industry.

Ed Farren

Oregon Cowboy

The Cascade Mountains divide Oregon into two very different kinds of land. On the west side are the forests, the green valleys, the flowing rivers. On the east is the desert.

Clouds roll in from the Pacific Ocean, moving east. They pour rain on the land and then rise, following the line of the mountains, losing moisture all the time. And then they float, undisturbed, over the desert.

To the west, where there is water, you will find the loggers. To the east, you find the cowboys.

"Unless you started in a racket like this, you never are any good at it. And—but you take a boy that's raised at it and he's a good cowboy—you learn to think, you're thinkin' all day long, you have to be thinkin'."

The cowboy is out there on the range, squeezing a living out of the dry earth. Cattleman John Lane is one of them. His family came here from Ireland.

"Well, my father came from County Kerry. Came to New York about 1912. Worked in a grocery store as a box boy until he got the price of the road to come west. And when he came west he got a job herding sheep. And from there he saved a little money and bought the first ranch he owned in 1918, which we still own."

John Lane is one of the few ranchers who still owns the land. Many who found it too hard to hold onto their ranches had to give them up. They went back to the Bureau of Land Management, which leases the land back to the ranchers. But, hard as it is, cattle ranching is almost as important to Oregon's economy as lumber.

In parts of east Oregon, the life of a rancher (such as John Lane, far right) is much the way it was in the early twentieth century.

USDA Forest Service, Photo by Jim Hughes

In Oregon, most ranches are run by families. They herd cattle with horses, not helicopters.

" . . . *People have an oil well or something in their backyards and they use this for a hobby. We don't. We make a living out of it. That's our livelihood. . . . Then you have these en-*

Portrait of America

vironmentalists come out and they say we don't belong there. Well, we've been there . . . all our lives. So it's kind of a hard pill to swallow when somebody back there'll tell you, 'Well, that's our land,' when all the relatives all the way back down fought for that land and held onto it."

It's strange how people who live their lives in a constant struggle with the land so often grow to love and respect it in a very special way. They depend on the land and know that it has to be taken care of and protected.

"You spend a lifetime developing up an area. You're not gonna quit and walk off. You built it up for everything: for your wildlife, for your cattle, for everybody that's there—you built it up. You're not gonna quit and walk away from it."

An Oregon cowboy in Hells Canyon.

Fresh Air, Art, and Flowers

When you think of the natural beauty and clean air of Oregon, it's not surprising that a lot of what Oregonians do, they do outdoors.

In the town of Ashland, they take their Shakespeare with a breath of fresh air. The Shakespeare Festival runs from June to September and is considered one of the best in the country. Actors come from all over to audition, to try for the opportunity to work in the fine productions presented in an open-air Elizabethan theater.

The audience sits outside, as audiences often did in England in the time of Shakespeare. Before the play, they watch Elizabethan dances performed to Shakespearean songs. The costumes are colorful. The dancing is elegant and lively.

Green Lakes Basin, in Deschutes County, with
Broken Top Mountain in the background.

And the plays are some of the best productions of Shakespeare's works that you'll see in the country.

Closer to American traditional art forms is the All Northwest Barber Shop Ballad Contest and Gay Nineties Festival in Forest Grove in late February. Barbershop quartets from all over the northwestern part of the country come together for a little close harmony in an atmosphere that recalls the turn of the century.

Flower festivals blossom in the Oregon garden. There's the Portland Rose Festival with its parade, and floats covered with roses. And the Rhododendron Festival in Florence. There's the Fleet of Flowers Memorial Service in Depoe Bay in late May.

The cowboy heritage is reflected in rodeos and barbecues. And then a lot of Oregonians simply go out into the mountains and the forested wilderness to enjoy nature.

There are eleven national forests in Oregon. There are thirteen areas set aside as national wilderness areas, to be kept in their natural state. Oregon has

State of Oregon Travel and Information Section

Several of the sights and sounds of Oregon: the Shakespeare Festival in Ashland (far right and above, right) . . . Multnomah Falls, near Portland (right) . . . and the Pendleton Round-Up (above).

230 state parks where people camp and hike, ski in the winter, and swim in the summer.

In Oregon, you can fish, hunt, explore underground caves. Or you can stop by Eugene in June for the Bach Summer Musical Festival and take your classical music, like your Shakespeare, under the vaulting roof of the sky.

Portrait of America

Not Your Ordinary Lawyers

Oregon attracts many people who are not satisfied with living ordinary lives. They are looking for a certain *quality* of life. In this state, where a high value is put on nature, they often find what they are looking for.

Chris Kittell and Lois Albright, a husband and wife, are a good example. They're lawyers, and they enjoy their work. But it isn't quite enough for them. They want, not just to play in the Oregon outdoors, but to

USDA Forest Service, Photo by Jim Hughes

The Pacific Ocean and Lois Albright on a fishing boat.

work there. So, in the summer, Chris and Lois are salmon fishers.

"The judge understands. He doesn't schedule us for cases or trials or motions during the summer. That's the time we fish. And when the summer's over, that's the time when we'll take care of other people's problems. And I really like it that way."

Things work out very well for the fishing lawyers. They couldn't be salmon fishers all the time. The salmon season is too short for anyone to make a living at it full-time. These days, with the salmon getting scarcer, the season is getting even shorter. But the summers on a fishing boat are important to Lois.

"I was predisposed to being an outdoor person. My family was never that way, and I grew up without camping, without fishing. If my parents ever saw me kill a fish, I'm sure they'd be amazed."

There isn't a lot of money in salmon fishing these days. But there is still the sea and the fresh air. There is hard work in the sun that makes you go home feeling a good kind of tired. For Chris Kittell and Lois Albright, there is a balance in their life.

"I don't think anybody is strictly money, in terms of wanting to fish. It's a milieu; it's an atmosphere; it's an environment; it's a way of life, to a certain extent. And I think that's really one of the reasons we moved to the coast of Oregon. You just can't do that, you know, in that many places."

A Future
Full of Possibilities

"The white men were many, and we could not hold our own with them. We were like deer. They were like grizzly bears. We had a small country. Their country was large. We were content to let things remain as the Great Spirit made them. They were not, and would change the rivers if they did not suit them."

These words of Chief Joseph, of the Nez Percé Indians, tell us something important about the future of Oregon. Europeans came into a state already rich and beautiful. They saw possibilities where the Indians had seen simply what was. Looking at a land in terms of its possibilities is an exciting and a dangerous thing.

The American settlers were not afraid to change the land, change the rivers. They built dams, irrigated, cut the forests. They put the land to use.

The skyline of Portland against Mount Hood.

Sea Lion Caves in Florence.

But there is a thin line between using and abusing. Today, the people of Oregon again are looking at a future full of possibilities. A land this rich can give them almost anything they want. But *what* do the Oregon people want? The wealth of possibilities makes that a difficult question to answer.

Some people feel that Oregon's best hope for the future lies in preserving as much as in using. They want more wilderness kept as it is. They want fewer trees cut and more planted.

Other people feel that the land is there to be used. Changing the rivers is part of that.

For people who live in other parts of the country, places where the wilderness has already been destroyed, the natural beauty of Oregon seems a rare and wonderful thing that should not be touched. But for the people of Oregon, the land is also their living. That makes the question more complicated.

And it is the people of Oregon who will have to decide. Among all the possibilities.

Important Historical Events in Oregon

1579 Sir Francis Drake of England may have landed on Oregon's coast. He was searching for a route from the northern Pacific to the Atlantic Ocean.

1778 The British explorer James Cook reaches Cape Foulweather, north of Yaquina Bay.

1792 George Vancouver of Great Britain explores and makes maps of the Oregon coast. Robert Gray sails the Columbia River and names it after his ship.

1805 Lewis and Clark journey overland to the mouth of the Columbia River.

1811 John Jacob Astor's Pacific Fur Company builds a trading post and founds Astoria, near the mouth of the Columbia River.

1819 Spain gives up its claim to land north of latitude 42°, today's southern border of Oregon.

1842 Russia gives up its claims south of latitude 54° 40'.

1843 An overland migration (about 1,000 people), arrives over the Oregon Trail. They settle in the Willamette Valley and set up a government at Champoeg.

1844 Agitation for U.S. control of Oregon makes "Fifty-four Forty or Fight" James K. Polk's presidential campaign slogan.

1846 A treaty with Great Britain makes 49° north latitude the dividing line between U.S. and British territory.

1848 The Oregon Territory is created. The capital is Oregon City.

1850 The Donation Land Law provides free land for settlers.

1853 The Washington Territory is created, establishing the boundaries of present-day Oregon.

1856 Chief John, the Indian leader, surrenders and is imprisoned.

1859 Oregon becomes the 33rd state, February 14. The capital is Salem.

1872 The Modoc War begins in November and lasts until June 1873.

1877 Chief Joseph leads Nez Percé Indians in rebelling against being moved from Wallowa Valley to a reservation in Idaho. He is defeated.

1902 Crater Lake National Park is created. "Initiative and referendum" is adopted; they are procedures that allow people to participate in making laws.

1912 Oregon gives women the right to vote.

1932 The Owyhee Dam is completed.

1937 Bonneville Dam is completed.

1955 A freeway between Portland and Salem is opened.

1964 Heavy floods damage western Oregon.

1965 The death penalty is abolished.

1967 Astoria Bridge, across the mouth of the Columbia River, links Oregon with Point Ellice, Washington.

1984 Construction to enlarge the power facilities of Bonneville Dam, located on the Columbia River, is completed.

Oregon Almanac

Nickname. The Beaver State.

Capital. Salem.

State Bird. Western Meadowlark.

State Flower. Oregon Grape.

State Tree. Douglas Fir.

State Motto. The Union.

State Song. Oregon, My Oregon.

State Abbreviations. Ore. or Oreg. (traditional); OR (postal).

Statehood. February 14th, 1859, the 33rd state.

Government. Congress: U.S. senators, 2; U.S. representatives, 5. **State Legislature** (Legislative Assembly): senators, 30; representatives, 60. **Counties:** 36.

Area. 96,981 sq. mi. (251,180 sq. km.), 10th in size among the states.

Greatest Distances. north/south, 295 mi. (475 km.); east/west, 375 mi. (603 km.). **Coastline:** 296 mi. (476 km.).

Elevation. Highest: Mount Hood, 11,239 ft. (3,426 m). **Lowest:** sea level, along the Pacific Ocean.

Population. 1980 Census: 2,632,663 (26% increase over 1970), 30th among the states. **Density:** 27 persons per sq. mi. (10 persons per sq. km.). **Distribution:** 68% urban, 32% rural. **1970 Census:** 2,091,533.

Economy. Agriculture: beef cattle, wheat, milk, greenhouse and nursery products, potatoes, forest products. **Fishing Industry:** salmon, tuna, shrimp. **Manufacturing:** lumber, wood products, food products, paper products, nonelectric machinery, transportation equipment, primary metals, fabricated metal products. **Mining:** sand and gravel, stone, nickel, pumice.

Places to Visit

Bonneville Dam.
Columbia River Gorge.
Picture Gorge.
Crater Lake National Park.
Oregon Caves National Monument.
Fort Clatsop National Memorial.

Annual Events

All Northwest Barber Shop Ballad Contest and Gay Nineties Festival in Forest Grove (February).

All-Indian Rodeo in Tygh Valley (May).

World Championship Timber Carnival in Albany (July).

Chief Joseph Days in Joseph (July).

State Fair in Salem (September-October).

Pacific International Livestock Exposition in Portland (November).

Oregon Counties

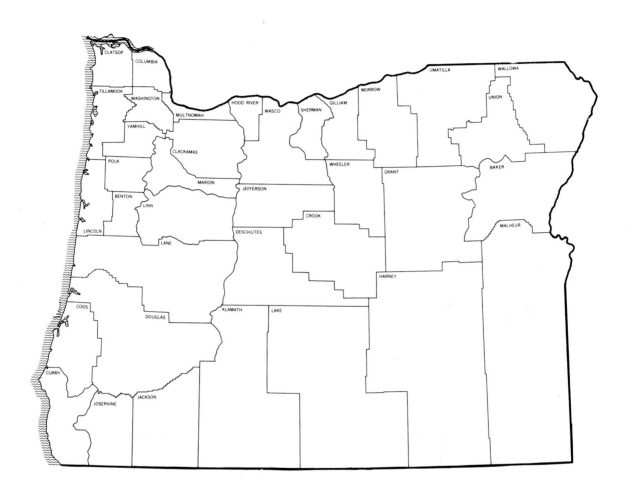

INDEX

979.5
THOMPSON

Thompson, Kathleen
Oregon

DATE DUE		
MAR 17		
MAR 29		
D-5		
MAR 21		
MAR 28		
APR 26		
SEP 20		